ADAPTED TO SURVIVE

ANIMALS THAT FLY

Angela Royston

Raintree

Chicago, Illinois

Edited by Dan Nunn, Rebecca Rissman, and Helen
Cox Cannons
Designed by Jo Hinton-Malivoire
Original illustrations © Capstone Global Library Ltd
Picture research by Mica Brancic
Production by Helen McCreath
Originated by Capstone Global Library Ltd
Printed and bound in China

17 16 15 14 13
10 9 8 7 6 5 4 3 2 1

**Library of Congress Cataloging-in-Publication
Data**
Royston, Angela, 1945- author.
  Animals that fly / Angela Royston.
    pages cm.—(Adapted to survive)
  Includes bibliographical references and index.
  ISBN 978-1-4109-6147-1 (hb)—ISBN 978-1-4109-
6154-9 (pb) 1. Animal flight—Juvenile literature. 2.
Animals—Adaptation—Juvenile literature. I. Title.
QL751.5.R694 2014
591.5′7—dc23   2013017631

Acknowledgments
The author and publisher are grateful to the
following for permission to reproduce copyright
material: Naturepl.com pp. 4 (© John Abbott), 5 (©
Ian McCarthy), 6 (© Peter Blackwell), 8 (© Bernard
Castelein), 9 (© Edwin Giesbers), 11 (Geslin/©
Wild Wonders of Europe), 12 (© Kevin Schafer), 13
(© Barry Mansell), 14 (Maitland/© Wild Wonders
of Europe), 15, 26 (© Stephen Dalton), 16 (© Rolf
Nussbaumer), 17 (© David Tipling), 18 (© Philip
Dalton), 19 (© Nick Upton), 21 (© Tui De Roy), 22,
29 bottom right (© Brent Stephenson), 23 (© David
Fleetham), 25 (© Kim Taylor), 27 (© Tim Laman);
Science Photo Library p. 10 (Steve Gschmeissner);
Shutterstock pp. 7 (© Igor Kovalenko), 20 (©
Christian Musat), 29 top right (© Rob van Esch),
29 top left (© niceregionpics), 24, 29 bottom left
(Minden Pictures).

Cover photograph of a Grey heron flying
reproduced with permission of Shutterstock
(© Neal Cooper).

We would like to thank Michael Bright for his
invaluable help in the preparation of this book.

Every effort has been made to contact copyright
holders of any material reproduced in this book.
Any omissions will be rectified in subsequent
printings if notice is given to the publisher.

All the Internet addresses (URLs) given in this
book were valid at the time of going to press.
However, due to the dynamic nature of the
Internet, some addresses may have changed,
or sites may have changed or ceased to exist
since publication. While the author and publisher
regret any inconvenience this may cause readers,
no responsibility for any such changes can be
accepted by either the author or the publisher.

Some words are shown in bold, **like this.** You can find
out what they mean by looking in the glossary.

CONTENTS

WHICH ANIMALS CAN FLY?

Birds and insects are the most common flying animals. Bats can also fly. Some animals, including fish, can **glide**! Why and how do animals fly?

beetle

Largest Flying Birds

The wandering albatross has the largest **wingspan** of all birds. Its wingspan can reach 11 feet (3½ meters) across.

WHY ANIMALS FLY

Animals fly for several reasons. Flying is a good way of getting from one place to another. Birds and insects fly away from danger on the ground. Insects fly from flower to flower to find food, and some birds catch insects as they fly.

This lion is trying to grab a vulture before it can fly away.

DID YOU KNOW?
Snow geese avoid the cold Arctic winter by flying south to a warmer country.

7

ADAPTED TO FLY

Adaptations are special things about an animal's body that help it **survive**. Flying animals have wings that lift and push them through the air. Birds and bats have strong wings made of bones, covered with feathers or skin. The wing bones are the same bones that form our arms and fingers.

Insect wings are made of very thin skin.

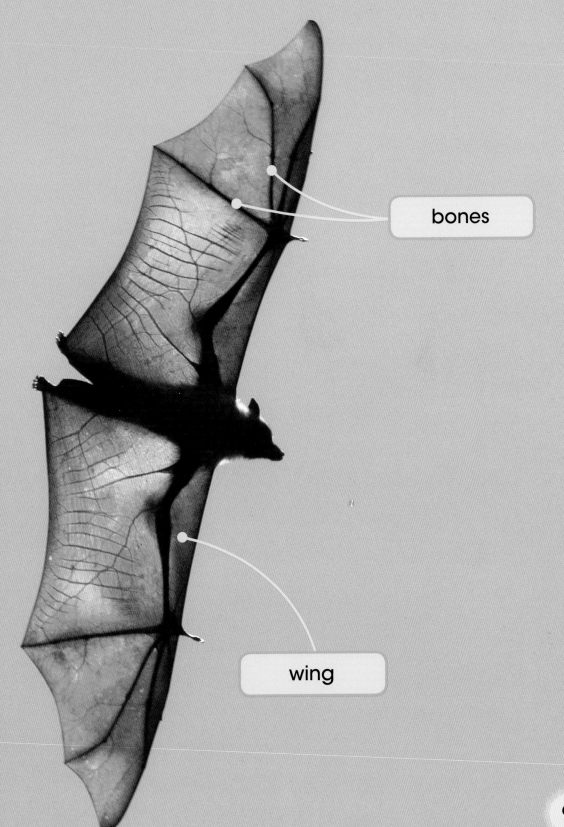

bones

wing

BIRD CHAMPIONS

As well as wings, birds have other **adaptations** that help them fly. Their bones and feathers are hollow, which makes them strong and light. Swifts can fly amazingly fast, at 69 miles (112 kilometers) per hour.

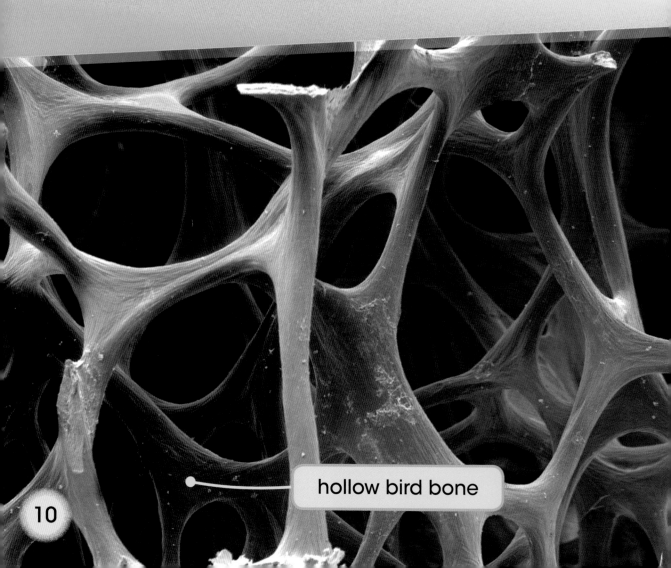

hollow bird bone

peregrine falcon diving

Peregrine falcons can dive at
a speed of around 200 miles
(320 kilometers) per hour.

BATS

A bat can change the shape of its wing as it flies. This allows the bat to change direction very fast. Bats find their way in the dark by making high-pitched squeaks and listening for the echoes. This **adaptation** is called echolocation.

DID YOU KNOW?
Bats hang upside down to sleep!

INSECTS

Most insects have two pairs of wings, which they beat very fast. Insects can quickly take off in any direction to escape from danger. Insects are so small that it is hard to measure exactly how fast they can fly. Desert locusts are probably the fastest fliers, at 20 miles (33 kilometers) per hour.

owlfly

dragonfly

HOVERING

Some birds can **hover**, or stay still in midair like a helicopter. Hummingbirds beat their wings very fast and hover while they sip **nectar** from flowers. **Birds of prey** hover, too. They fly into the wind and use their wings to stay in the same place.

Kites watch for **prey** on the ground, and then they dive to grab it!

HOVERING INSECTS

Some insects, such as hoverflies, can **hover**, too. Hummingbird hawkmoths hover like hummingbirds to feed from flowers. They have a long **proboscis**, which they use like a straw. This **adaptation** allows them to suck **nectar** from tube-shaped flowers.

DID YOU KNOW?
Hummingbird hawkmoths beat
their wings so fast that they hum!

proboscis

GLIDING

Birds **glide** when they move through the air without flapping their wings. Gliding takes less energy than flying, so large birds often glide. For example, albatrosses, vultures, eagles, and storks are good gliders.

Birds that glide have long, large wings.

stork

condor

Ace Glider
A condor uses rising warm air to help it glide. It may flap its wings only once every hour to keep going!

FLYING FISH

Flying fish have large side **fins** that act like wings. The fish leap out of the water and **glide** to escape from ocean **predators**. A flying fish can glide for up to 45 seconds and cover up to 1,312 feet (400 meters).

Amazing Fish
A flying fish pushes its tail against the water as it drops down. This helps it lift up again.

FLYING SQUIRRELS

Flying squirrels live in trees. A flying squirrel has a large flap of furry skin between the front and back legs on each side of its body. This **adaptation** allows it to **glide** from tree to tree. A flying squirrel uses its flat tail to help itself steer.

A flying squirrel thrusts its feet forward to slow itself down before it lands.

FLYING DRAGONS

A flying dragon is a lizard that lives in trees. Its "wings" are flaps of skin attached to extra-long **rib** bones on each side of its body. It can **glide** for up to 30 feet (9 meters) from one tree to another. It uses its tail to help it steer.

DID YOU KNOW?
A flying dragon folds away its wings when it is not gliding.

ANIMAL CHALLENGE

1. Do you think small wings or big wings are better for flying long distances?

2. Cats climb trees but do not **glide**. What **adaptation** would they need to glide?

3. Why can't penguins fly through the air?

Invent your own flying animal. You can use some of the adaptations shown in the photos or make up your own.

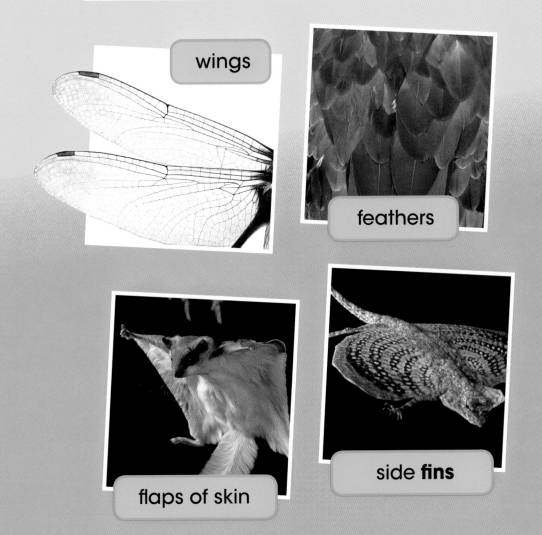

wings

feathers

flaps of skin

side **fins**

Answers to Animal Challenge

1. Big wings are better for flying long distances, because they provide more lift.

2. In order to glide, one adaptation that would help a cat would be to have flaps of skin that stretch between the front and back legs.

3. A penguin is too heavy and its wings are too small for it to fly through the air. Instead, it uses its wings as flippers to swim through the water.

GLOSSARY

adaptation special thing about an animal's body that helps it survive in a particular way or in a particular habitat

bird of prey bird that hunts and eats small animals, such as mice and other birds

fins stiff flaps that stick out from a fish's body to help the fish move and steer

glide move through the air without flapping wings

hover hang in the air without moving forward or backward

nectar sweet juice made inside some flowers

predator animal that hunts and kills other animals for food

prey animal that is hunted and eaten by another animal

proboscis long tube through which an insect or other animal sucks up liquid

rib one of a number of curved bones that protect the heart of an animal

survive manage to go on living

wingspan distance from one wingtip to the other when the wings are stretched open

FIND OUT MORE

BOOKS

DiCostanzo, Joseph. *What's That Bird? A Beginner's Guide.* New York: DK Publishing, 2012.

Guillain, Charlotte. *Bats* (Animal Abilities). Chicago: Raintree, 2014.

Slade, Suzanne. *Birds: Winged and Feathered Animals.* Mankato, Minn.: Picture Window, 2010.

Thomas, Isabel. *Brilliant Birds* (Extreme Animals). Chicago: Raintree, 2013.

WEB SITES

FactHound offers a safe, fun way to find Internet sites related to this book. All of the sites on FactHound have been researched by our staff.

Here's all you do:
Visit www.facthound.com
Type in this code: 9781410961471

INDEX